AS Geography
UNIT 2

Specification **B**

Unit 2: Managing Change in Human Environments

Sue Warn

Philip Allan Updates
Market Place
Deddington
Oxfordshire
OX15 0SE

tel: 01869 338652
fax: 01869 337590
e-mail: sales@philipallan.co.uk
www.philipallan.co.uk

ISBN-13: 978-0-86003-467-4
ISBN-10: 0-86003-467-4

This Guide has been written specifically to support students preparing for the Edexcel Specification B AS Geography Unit 2 examination. The content has been neither approved nor endorsed by Edexcel and remains the sole responsibility of the author.

Typeset by Magnet Harlequin, Oxford
Printed by Information Press, Eynsham, Oxford

Contents

Introduction

■ ■ ■

Content Guidance

■ ■ ■

Questions and Answers

Introduction

About this guide

The purpose of this guide is to help you understand what is required to do well in **Unit 2: Changing Human Environments**. (The full content details are on pages 22–25 of the Edexcel specification. Your teacher or lecturer will have a copy of this.)

The guide is divided into three sections.

This **Introduction** explains the structure of the guide and the importance of finding linkages between rural and urban environments, and between the AS and A2 parts of the course. It also provides some general advice on how to approach the unit test.

The **Content Guidance** section sets out the *bare essentials* of the Unit 2 specification, which comprises two sub-units — rural environments and urban environments. A series of diagrams is used to help your understanding; many are simple to draw and could be used in the exam.

This section helps you develop essential skills such as responding to data and using case studies. The review exercises help you to test your understanding of difficult areas. There are also some tips on how to tackle these exercises and how to approach your revision.

The **Question and Answer** section includes three sample exam questions in the style of the unit test paper. Sample answers at C and A grade are provided, as well as examiner's comments on how to tackle each question and on where marks are gained or lost in the sample answers.

Linkages

You should try to make linkages between the rural and urban sub-units.
- There are **physical** linkages, in that rural and urban environments are connected in a rural–urban continuum, and through processes such as urbanisation and counter-urbanisation.
- There are **parallel** linkages — for example, both systems are in a state of change, both spatially and over time. As one changes so does the other.
- There are **process** linkages, in that similar processes brought about by population dynamics, migration and economic development produce short-term and long-term changes and conflicts.

AS Unit 2 also forms a foundation for A2 study. As part of A2, the final **Unit 6** is a *synoptic exercise*. You are given a series of resources about a geographical issue within an area and then, under exam conditions, you have to use these resources to carry out a structured inquiry, considering a number of planning choices for the area. Clearly, if the resources are for a rural or urban area, you need to revisit Unit 2.

As this synoptic exercise is testing your ability to draw together what you have learnt (knowledge, understanding and skills) from all the AS/A2 units, you need to be making these linkages throughout the course.

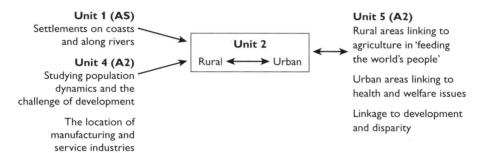

General advice on AS unit tests

Choice of questions

You must answer any three of the five questions set. To help you find them, topics will appear in the same order as in the specification: (1) and (2) are questions on rural environments, (3) is a mixed rural–urban question, and (4) and (5) are questions on urban environments.

Always look at the whole question before making your final choice. The mini-essay at the end of each question is worth 10 marks (33%), so don't make your choice based only on the resources, or you may get a shock.

Timing

The examination lasts for 1 hour 30 minutes. Each question is worth 30 marks, so you have to earn 'a mark every minute'. If you can't answer a subsection, just miss it out and go straight on. You can go back later.

You must answer three complete questions. For the short answers, bullet points are quite acceptable, but the mini-essay expects extended writing. However, even here, notes are better than nothing. Try to write detailed, factual prose, and not to waste words. Make every word count.

Quality of written communication

For both the AS examination papers, up to 4 marks are added on according to:
• the quality of your spelling (if you are dyslexic, seek special consideration)

- your punctuation and grammar
- the structure and ordering of your response into a logical answer
- appropriate use of geographical terminology

Concepts and geographical terms

It is a good idea to compile a list of key ideas and terms as you meet them. You might refer to other books (your teacher will have a vocabulary list in their *Teacher's Guide*) and there are many such terms throughout this book (in bold type).

Managing questions

Go through each subsection lightly underlining or ringing key words. In particular, look for:

- command words (e.g. 'describe', 'identify', 'examine')
- locations (e.g. is LEDC or MEDC specified?)
- the number of reasons or answers required (e.g. *two* ways, *one* reason, etc.)
- 'with the aid of a diagram' — this means you must draw one if you want full marks

Judge the length of your answer. The lines provided on your paper are a guide for writing of an average size. You can write more if you wish, with no penalties, and don't be afraid to draw a diagram — it doesn't matter that there are lines on the paper.

Content Guidance

Unit 2 comprises two sub-units:
- **rural environments**
- **urban environments**

Note that the unit emphasises rural–urban linkages, spatially and over time.

In this Content Guidance section, after an introduction to the rural–urban continuum, each of these sub-units has the following structure:
- key characteristics of the environment
- processes leading to change in the environment
- managing key issues in the environment — this is an applied geography section in which you explore planning and management issues
- looking ahead to the future — in particular, reviewing the feasibility and economic viability of more sustainable strategies

This unit requires you to study environments in a variety of locations experiencing different states of development. Therefore, in each section, processes and key issues are explored in MEDCs and LEDCs.

The rural–urban continuum

Rural and urban environments are closely linked to each other, for example, through food supply, and work or leisure activities. It is very difficult to distinguish between rural and urban environments by a single feature. In reality there is a **rural–urban continuum**. This section looks at a number of criteria you can use to distinguish between rural and urban areas.

Size

Many countries employ a **population threshold**, for example of 20000 people, for a settlement to be classed as urban, but the threshold value varies between countries and much depends on the character of the area. In sparsely populated areas, such as western Canada or Sweden, a settlement of 1000 people may be much more urban in character than an agro-town of 30000 people in a densely populated area of Nigeria. The range of minimum populations is from 200 in Norway to 50000 in Japan. For a parish to be classed as rural in the UK, the Countryside Commission suggests it should contain fewer than 10000 people.

Function

Urban areas have a wide range of functions, such as cultural activity, retailing, education and finance. These functions are of a higher order (level) in urban areas, for example a department store or a college as opposed to a village store or a primary school. Urban areas, therefore, are central places and they have a sphere of influence. In contrast, rural areas usually have comparatively few services, and most of these are concentrated in a small market town — an urban island in a sea of rurality!

Employment

Traditionally, the main source of employment in urban areas is either in the secondary (manufacturing) or in the tertiary (services) sectors. These urban areas attract many employees from their catchment area. There is little, if any, primary activity in urban areas in more economically developed countries (MEDCs). However, in urban areas of many less economically developed countries (LEDCs), there are urban farms that people develop to support themselves. These towns are called agro-towns.

Many countries, such as Israel, use an upper limit of percentage employed in agriculture as part of the urban definition (usually 15–25%). However, in rural areas in MEDCs less than 20% may work in primary activities (it can be as low as 2%), while in LEDCs over 80% of the population might be subsistence farmers.

Density

Urban areas are built-up. Therefore, **threshold population densities** can be used as a measure of this built-up nature. The usual range is from 100–400 people per km^2.

Rural areas can contain over 1000 people per km^2 (e.g. Java in Indonesia) but are frequently sparsely populated.

Administration

Many urban areas function as centres of government. In some countries (e.g. Iraq) a particular government function confers the status of urban, and all areas within the municipality councils are designated as urban. Equally, other councils are declared to be rural, district or parish councils, which have responsibility for few services.

Character

People like to suggest that urban areas have a social dimension — an urban lifestyle (**urbanism**) that is characterised by pace, stress and a desire to be upwardly mobile. Urban environments are also characterised by a more obvious polarisation from extreme wealth to acute poverty within small areas. On the other hand, people perceive rural environments as stress-free, with a slow pace of life — a rural idyll. However, rural environments in MEDCs do contain pockets of poverty while in LEDCs there can be large regions of extreme rural poverty.

The rural–urban continuum covers a **hierarchy** of settlements, as shown below.

Isolated dwelling → farm → hamlet → village → large village → subtown → town → large town → city → large city → conurbation → megalopolis or world city

All the characteristics become more extreme the higher the position in the hierarchy. For example, a village might offer a primary school and a pub while a city might offer specialist cultural facilities, a university and a number of regional offices. These high-order functions give the city a very large sphere of influence. Obviously, the higher up the hierarchy the fewer the number of settlements.

Rural environments

How and why do rural environments vary in landscape and character?

So far we have identified the essential differences *between* rural and urban areas. However, there is enormous variety *within* rural environments. You can imagine a continuum, ranging from wildscapes in remote rural areas (RRAs) to urbanised landscapes in the rural–urban fringe of accessible rural areas (ARAs) that have many suburban characteristics. This continuum is changing as the world is gradually becoming more urbanised. Figure 1 explains some of the reasons for *variety* within rural areas.

Changes in rural population and settlements

Although, in general, remote rural areas lost population in the period 1930–1970, in most MEDCs, accessible rural areas gained population, essentially as a result of movement of both population and employment from central urban areas. The movement was facilitated by improved public transport and increased ownership of private cars. From 1970, as **counterurbanisation** began to take place, most rural districts began to experience an upsurge in population known as the **rural turnround**. Rural areas (even more remote areas) increased their population by an average of 16% between 1971 and 1991, in contrast to metropolitan cities, where populations decreased by 18% in the same period. Tables 4 and 5 show the population changes in South Molton Rural District in north Devon.

Table 4 Push and pull factors affecting migrants
in South Molton Rural District

Reasons	For leaving ('push') (%)	For choosing South Molton ('pull') (%)
Economic reasons		
Move required by employer	10	0
Voluntary career move	12	29
Unemployment	10	0
Housing/property	5	54
Total economic reasons	**37**	**83**
Non-economic reasons		
Lifestyle change	23	0
Retirement	14	0
Family health	11	8
Social and physical reasons	10	8
Total non-economic reasons	**58**	**16**
Other reasons	5	1

Table 5 Population change in South Molton Rural District, 1951–91

Measures of change	1951–61	1961–71	1971–81	1981–91
Population change (number)	−1041	−93	1790	1753
Population change (%)	−9	−1	16	13
Number of parishes with increasing population	2	9	24	23
Number of parishes with decreasing population	27	20	5	6

South Molton is a small town in rural north Devon, just south of the Exmoor National Park. It lies about 20 km inland from Barnstaple. The M5 motorway is about 50 km away to the east.

Source: Devon County Council

19

The tables illustrate a number of points:
- the increase in population arose because of in-migration, for reasons such as the push and pull factors (note the importance of housing and lifestyle change)
- the turnround took place *after* 1971
- the rural district shows considerable variation between parishes, with the majority increasing (usually **key settlements** with a range of basic services and good accessibility to commuting routes), although a minority declined

Demographics also play a part in influencing increases/decreases, as shown in Figure 5, which illustrates how household turnover is taking place.

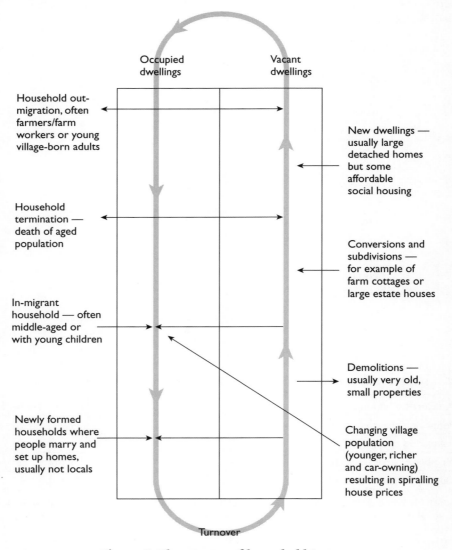

Figure 5 The process of household turnover

Changes in employment have occurred in many villages. These can be viewed in three ways:

- how employment has changed *nationally* in MEDCs (**sector theory**). Over time primary employment declines at the expense initially of manufacturing and ultimately of tertiary (services) employment
- how employment may have changed *regionally*, with many 'new' arrivals to villages commuting to market towns for work
- how employment may have changed *locally* in a particular village. While many of the newcomers' jobs may be outside the village, **rural manufacturing** is a rapidly growing sector. The rural economy is now as diverse as the national economy. **Small businesses** form the backbone of the rural economy. In the UK, a higher percentage of people in rural areas are self-employed (15%) and a higher percentage of adults in employment work from home (**teleworking**) than nationally

As we saw in the rural district of South Molton, while most villages are expanding, some are declining in terms of population. Growth or decline is quite complex to sort out because quite often settlements have periods of both. Equally, some settlements, such as Urchfont in Wiltshire, are not really growing *numerically* but the population is *changing* by the process of household turnover (see Figure 5), and a younger population may lead to future growth.

Tip Either from fieldwork or from textbooks, draw two sketch maps of a growing village and a declining village in terms of population. Annotate them to show the pattern of growth and decline and the reasons for it. Consider how changes in population are linked to changes in housing, services and employment.

Review 3

Study Figure 5. Explain how the process of household turnover is leading to changes in population structure, village services and village employment.

Tables 6 and 7 show the impact of rural change on rural services.

Table 6 Percentages of parishes without certain services, 2000

Worsening situation compared with 1991	Apparently stable situation	Improving situation compared with 1991
Permanent shop (42%) Post office (43%) Seven-day bus service (75%) Bank or building society (91%) Police station (92%)	*Pub (29%) Petrol station *GP surgery (85%)	Village hall or similar (28%) Bottle bank or recycling scheme (60%) Community minibus or social car scheme (79%) Public or private nursery (86%) Daycare for elderly people (91%)
*Other evidence suggests a decline in the number of pubs and surgeries in the 1990s		

Table 7 Why have rural services declined and why might they improve?

	The bad news	The good news
Food shops	• Supermarkets opening even in quite small towns, with lower prices, extended hours and free buses from some villages	• Relief from uniform business rates • Development of new types of village shops, e.g. farm and garage shops
Post offices	• Small offices downgraded to part-time community office status — unattractive as going concerns for people to run • Diversion of pensions business to banks	• New deals for rural post offices with banks, with the post office counters for general new business
Public transport	• Bus deregulation led to closure of uneconomic routes • New unitary councils subsidise their own services, not rural cross-council links • Not enough passengers	• Grants for community taxis and buses which are often developed by parish councils
Village schools	• Ageing population leads to a lack of 'customers' • As schools compete for numbers the tendency is for children not to attend their local village school, or they go 'private'	• Development of nurseries • Generally good performance of small schools encourages numbers • Clustering strategies for a shared headteacher • Government grants for small schools
Libraries	• Cost of provision • Cuts in council services	• Increased mobile libraries
Primary healthcare	• Closure of GP 'branch' surgeries • Decline in NHS dentistry • Essentially escalating NHS costs	• Creation of mini health centres • Extra grants for rural GPs • Development of rural pharmacies • Use of internet for consultations
Village halls	• General trends of changing family habits • Withdrawal of funding for youth clubs and social services	• Millennium grants for refurbishment

Review 4

Use Tables 6 and 7 to assess the impact of rural change on rural services. Explain why it is not all bad news.

Figure 6 summarises the possible effects of population decline and population expansion on a village.

Managing rural poverty and deprivation

Of the rural problems to be tackled, poverty is perhaps the most fundamental, particularly in LEDCs, but rural poverty can also be a problem in MEDCs.

Rural areas in MEDCs are largely regarded as more affluent than urban areas, but they contain a significant proportion of poorer people, scattered thinly, with small pockets of severe deprivation. Because of the smallness of these groups, and the perception of rural areas as idylls, they can be easily hidden.

In the UK, average incomes are in general higher in rural areas than in urban areas. However, some peripheral rural districts such as those in Cornwall — now eligible for Category 1 EU funding (the most extreme hardship) — have the lowest average earnings of anywhere in Britain. Equally, while unemployment is generally lower in rural areas, finding employment can be difficult for school leavers. There is often a limited range of job opportunities because of physical constraints, and much employment (around 27%) is part time and, therefore, lower paid.

Rural areas also include a greater proportion of elderly people (nearly 20%) and while housing in rural areas is generally of a higher standard, there is little affordable housing in village areas. The poverty of these mainly aged 'rural folk' can be extreme, especially when it is combined with deprivation of access to basic services, and the fact that people are less willing to declare their needs. Rural **social exclusion** exists, where people are excluded from social, economic or cultural opportunities because of low income, poverty, poor health or reduced access to services.

Definitions
- **Rural disadvantage** is the inability of individuals or households to share in lifestyles open to the majority.
- **Rural poverty** is the inability of individuals or households to share in lifestyles open to the majority because of a lack of financial resources. Usually a threshold income is stated but this will of course differ between MEDCs and LEDCs.
- **Rural deprivation** is usually associated with a lack of material resources and is really a 'state of non-wellbeing' to include impacts on physical and mental health caused by this lack.
- **Social exclusion** is the process whereby the various systems that should guarantee the social integration of individuals or households fail to do so. Examples include the failure of employment provision or the housing markets.

Rural deprivation takes three forms:
- **Household deprivation** is concerned with the hardships of individual households trying to maintain a living standard. The plight of tenant farmers in less-favoured areas, such as the Welsh mountains, or that of elderly single people solely dependent on their state pensions are examples. Household deprivation may be typified by poor-quality housing and high levels of income support and benefit payments.
- **Opportunity deprivation** is concerned with country dwellers' lack of access to education, health, work, social services and shops. Many rural families have to

.face the expense and difficulty of travelling longer distances even for basic services such as fuel — and paying more for them.

- **Mobility deprivation** is a measure of the lack of transport for going to work or for obtaining basic services, many of which are now concentrated in key settlements because of rural rationalisation. Owning a car or motorbike is extremely expensive, especially for low-income families. Access to a village taxi, post-bus or community bus service can be vital in the absence of commercial bus services. This was the number one issue raised by the 1999 WI survey.

The impact of a lack of transport on rural life is shown in Figure 9.

(1) Since the village bus service was axed, young Jack Norris has had to leave his home and friends in order to live nearer his job, 12 miles away. It's a shame the way the old place keeps losing so many of its young people

(2) The village bus service was so handy for Mrs Payne. It meant that whatever she couldn't buy in the village, she could always get in the next town. Now there's no bus, she's got a problem (not to mention a 3 mile walk). Mrs Payne does not have a driving licence

(3) Like a lot of young people today, Alan Murphy can't get a job. And now, he doesn't even have the means to go after one, because he's got no bus service either. No bus. No job. No hope

(4) Mrs Sarah Smith (68 last birthday) used to rely on the village bus to take her to the doctor's surgery. Now the bus service has gone, she has to beg a lift or take a 6 mile hike

(5) Ted Armitage hasn't been on a bus in years. Hasn't needed to with the car. But he's far from happy about the effect the lack of a bus service is having on the village. Ted runs the local shop — and it's not good for business the way people keep packing up and leaving

(6) It's not Jane Harding's fault that her new secondary school is $2\frac{1}{2}$ miles away from the village. But it's her problem, because Jane's parents can't afford to run a car and the bus that took her to school has run its last journey. Now she has to bike it, and that's not much fun in the winter

(7) Tracey Cole is 17 and she's had it with village life. There was never much to do there anyway, but now the bus service has gone, she and her mates feel marooned. Never mind what her parents say, she's off to the bright lights and the big city just as soon as her bags are packed

Figure 9 An everyday story of country folk

The combined impact of the various facets of deprivation is shown in Figure 10. It can, unless arrested, cause a cycle of **rural decline**. This can lead to rural **depopulation** if the people lost by out-migration are not replaced by new incomers.

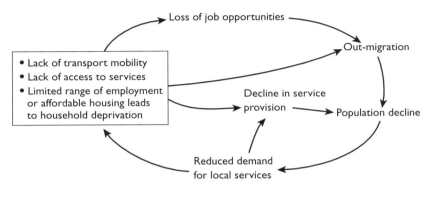

Figure 10

Solutions — a UK case study (similar schemes exist throughout the EU)

In the UK and many other MEDCs, governments are keen to recognise the problems of the countryside, especially the loss of vital services, the lack of a range of quality jobs, and the lack of affordable housing. The problem is how to encourage rural development while still protecting the rural environment and conserving the rural character of the areas.

In the period up to 2000, support for rural areas was provided in a number of ways:
- the creation of **rural development areas** (fund priority areas) for regions that have been experiencing particular social and economic problems, and so qualify for grants towards developing and improving employment (new rural industrial estates, tourist ventures, extending training opportunities etc.), for example Cornwall, North Pennines
- **rural challenge grants** can be awarded after competition for imaginative and effective solutions to tackle a particular problem, for example lack of a particular service could be solved by a multipurpose centre
- **EU funding** is particularly significant for Cornwall (the poorest region), while the **European Regional Fund** and other structural funding is available for community initiatives
- specific targeted strategies, for example the **Rural Transport Partnership Scheme** (aimed at producing quality bus partnerships) and the **Village Shop Development Scheme**
- funds for sustainable development initiatives run by voluntary organisations
- the **Millennium Fund**, which was developed to renovate village halls and community centres (over 90% of villages now have a quality community focal point)

The Countryside Agency was formed in 1999 to draw together a range of countryside initiatives. Its vision for the future is shown in Figure 11.

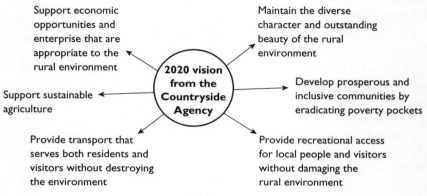

Figure 11

After strong criticism in the press that it was neglecting the needs of rural people and the countryside, the Labour government consulted widely and produced a second rural White Paper (2000). Specific proposals were designed to empower local people and included the following:

- revitalising small subtowns and market towns with a £37 million cash boost to help them develop a new role for themselves as key service centres, i.e. to ensure rural dwellers are guaranteed services within a reasonable journey distance
- providing new funding for rural buses to support bus routes for rural dwellers and visitors (includes village taxis, dial-a-ride and community buses)
- providing even more support for diversity in farming and the development of high-quality regional and local products (specialist cheeses etc.)
- building more affordable homes in rural areas to stem the outward flow of young, village-born people
- targeting rural people who suffer social exclusion, through better information and more tailored programmes of support
- ensuring improved protection of the countryside by making better use of brown-field sites, thus taking pressure off greenfield sites and reducing the need to build on farmland
- providing more money and better management for National Parks and areas of outstanding natural beauty (AONBs), with stronger planning protection for AONBs
- safeguarding and improving village services, including pubs and shops and child-care, through a £15 million Community Service Fund, run by the Countryside Agency
- a Rural Charter to guarantee the quality of rural services
- enabling more people to enjoy the countryside through new legal access and a better rights-of-way network

Together these proposals are known as the **Blueprint for Revival**.

Tip Use the Countryside Agency's website, www.countryside.gov.uk, to obtain details of examples of the latest initiatives. Find your local county council's website to obtain details of its Agenda 21 Sustainable Rural Initiatives. Case studies of such initiatives are vital to support your extended writing questions. Try to be as up to date as possible.

Rural poverty in LEDCs

Some stark facts from the 1999 UN Human Development Report are that:

- 841 million people worldwide are malnourished
- 13.2 million people worldwide are refugees
- desertification and drought affect 1.5 billion people worldwide
- 1.3 billion people in LEDCs live on less than US$1 a day
- 6–8 hours a day are spent by rural women in LEDCs fetching clean water and fuel wood
- 880 million people worldwide have no access to health services
- 38 million people live with HIV
- 109 million school-age children never go to school (they are required to work for the family income)
- 885 million adults worldwide are illiterate
- 14 million children in LEDCs die before they reach 5 years of age

These are the facts about poverty in LEDCs and much of this poverty occurs in rural areas. Figure 12 summarises the main effects of the cycle of rural poverty in subsistence economies, which stem from an inability of people to provide themselves with adequate food. There are long-term problems of malnourishment and shorter-term disasters such as those generated by the climate uncertainties of El Niño or enhanced global warming. The floods in Mozambique and the drought in Ethiopia were examples in 2000 where the delicate equilibrium of a decade of economic development was overturned.

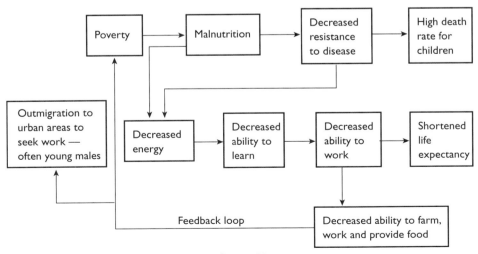

Figure 12

Considerable discussion occurs among development experts as to how best to raise living standards in LEDCs, especially in some of the more remote rural areas where environmental conditions are harsh and constraints enormous. Much governmental and World Bank aid has been for funding large capital projects, such as mega-dams, which are supposed to be multipurpose catalysts to regional development, or large-scale projects such as the Polonoroeste Project in Rondonia State, Brazil. The wealth generated from **top-down** projects in theory trickles down to the poorer peripheral areas. Many of these projects, in fact, make the lives of the rural poor worse rather than better. The reality is that in order to raise the living standards of the remote rural areas, **bottom-up** small-scale projects tend to work better, as the development is initiated in consultation with local people and is more targeted to local needs.

Table 8 lists the features of bottom-up development and identifies some examples — largely funded by NGOs.

Table 8

Features of bottom-up development (run by local people for local people)	Examples
Grants greater self-determination to rural areas; equitable communal decision-making; often small scale and tailored to local needs	Grameen Bank in Bangladesh, which has developed simple loan procedures for the rural poor
Uses limited funding effectively to make a difference	Many NGO projects (e.g. Water Aid)
Gives priority to projects that serve basic needs — health, education	Rural health programmes (e.g. barefoot doctor); basic school programmes in Tanzania; health projects (e.g. inoculation programme in Ethiopia)
Gives land to the people by land reform	Land reform in Tanzania, Zimbabwe or Cuba
Selects regionally appropriate technology	Farm Africa projects in Sudan and Kenya; rural blacksmith development in Gambia; IT development group projects worldwide (e.g. Kerala fishermen project, India); water tank scheme, Uganda
External physical resources are only used where peripheral/local ones are inadequate	Soil conservation strategies; water management plans in the Sahel area
Improvement of rural-to-urban and internal village communications	Village telephone/mobile telephone and cyber centre projects in northern India
Mobilises local indigenous human resources to create employment and increase productive activities (labour-intensive favoured)	Traidcraft projects in India, Bangladesh and Nepal (e.g. knitting cooperatives); small-scale enterprises in Malawi (UNCDF); CAFOD Working in Partnership scheme in Mozambique
Development projects emphasise the need to work with local environments and culture, and are sustainable	Ecotourism projects in Ecuador (Sacha Mama), Trinidad, Cape Yorke, Australia; Action Aid projects in Tarata, Peru or Altiplano in Bolivia

content guidance

Global urbanisation — understanding variations over time and in space

There is a very close relationship between economic development and urbanisation. Figure 17 shows a theoretical model of the process of urbanisation that countries follow to a lesser or greater degree over time.

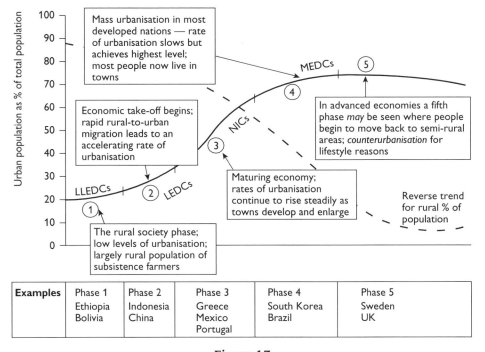

Examples	Phase 1	Phase 2	Phase 3	Phase 4	Phase 5
	Ethiopia	Indonesia	Greece	South Korea	Sweden
	Bolivia	China	Mexico	Brazil	UK
			Portugal		

Figure 17

In the eighteenth century most of the present-day MEDCs, such as the UK or Germany, experienced the Industrial Revolution, based on coalfields with extensive manufacturing industries. It took around 150 years for the urban percentage of the population to rise from 20% to 75%. The rates of urbanisation were slowed because of high death rates, with low life-expectancy (problems of tuberculosis, cholera etc.) and very high infant mortality.

In the twentieth century most current newly industrialised countries (NICs), such as the Asian tigers, completed the urbanisation curve (with the urban percentage of the population rising from 30% to 80%) in a matter of 50 years.

In theory, current LEDCs would be expected to complete the urbanisation curve very rapidly, but there are huge differentials in their rates of urban growth. In many cases countries are experiencing urbanisation without industrialisation, but because of the availability of basic medical care the actual rates of growth of urban population are far higher than those of eighteenth-century urbanisation.

In some least less economically developed countries (LLEDCs), the very poorest nations of the world, levels of urban population remain relatively low. This is because of the slow pace of development, and the realisation by people that they will be unable to feed themselves and buy essentials such as fuel if they move to towns. This applies to countries such as Ethiopia and Bolivia. In sub-Saharan Africa, the decimation of the population from AIDS in the cities of countries such as Uganda, Botswana and South Africa will also slow the rates of urbanisation as both natural increase and migration rates have been affected.

Looking at the situation **spatially**, Figure 18 is a 'freeze frame' or 'snapshot' of the global pathway of urbanisation. It shows how the countries of the world are distributed along the urbanisation curve at a particular time, in this case in the year 2000. Note the contrasts between the North and the South.

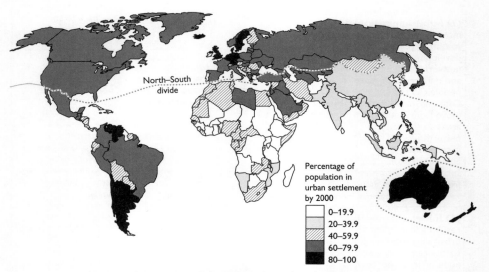

Figure 18 The global situation in 2000

Review 7

Write a systematic description of the pattern shown in Figure 18. (Hint: work through the key from high to low, always quoting named countries. Use the North–South divide as an introduction.)

Urbanisation — the growth of millionaire and mega-cities

Increased global urbanisation has resulted in the development of many larger **millionaire cities**. There are now a significant number of enormous **mega cities**, some of which are classed as world cities. These categories are defined as follows:

- millionaire cities (also known as million cities) are those with over 1 million people (these are now very common in China and India, the two most populated countries in the world)

- mega cities are those whose populations are over 5 million, or even 10 million which is now often used as the threshold (London is not technically a mega city)
- world cities are those that are truly influential on a global scale because of their financial status and worldwide commercial influence and power (e.g. London)

Urban processes — the cycle of urbanisation

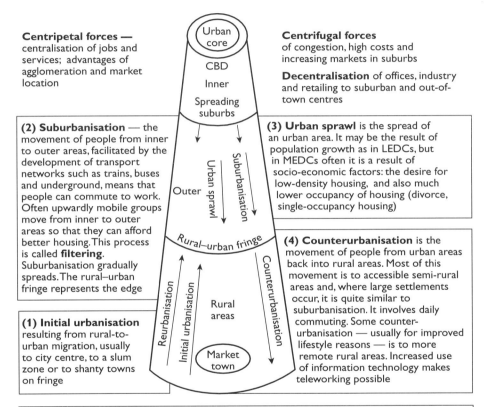

Centripetal forces — centralisation of jobs and services; advantages of agglomeration and market location

Centrifugal forces of congestion, high costs and increasing markets in suburbs

Decentralisation of offices, industry and retailing to suburban and out-of-town centres

(2) Suburbanisation — the movement of people from inner to outer areas, facilitated by the development of transport networks such as trains, buses and underground, means that people can commute to work. Often upwardly mobile groups move from inner to outer areas so that they can afford better housing. This process is called **filtering**. Suburbanisation gradually spreads. The rural–urban fringe represents the edge

(3) Urban sprawl is the spread of an urban area. It may be the result of population growth as in LEDCs, but in MEDCs often it is a result of socio-economic factors: the desire for low-density housing, and also much lower occupancy of housing (divorce, single-occupancy housing)

(4) Counterurbanisation is the movement of people from urban areas back into rural areas. Most of this movement is to accessible semi-rural areas and, where large settlements occur, it is quite similar to suburbanisation. It involves daily commuting. Some counter-urbanisation — usually for improved lifestyle reasons — is to more remote rural areas. Increased use of information technology makes teleworking possible

(1) Initial urbanisation resulting from rural-to-urban migration, usually to city centre, to a slum zone or to shanty towns on fringe

(5) Reurbanisation involves a range of processes which enable people and economic activities to move back to city centres. **Gentrification** is when middle-class people move back to run-down inner urban areas and improve the housing stock. Some reurbanisation results from planned initiatives such as those from Urban Development Corporations where inner central areas are improved in a number of ways, with high-value housing, hi-tech employment and improved environments

The cycle of urbanisation
- (1–5) is the typical sequence of processes in an MEDC.
- (1–3) is the sequence in most LEDC cities thus far.
- The processes result from the balance of centrifugal and centripetal forces. If there is outward movement, centrifugal forces are dominant.
- In some MEDC cities centrifugal forces have become so strong that planners are working to regenerate the centripetal forces.

Figure 19

The precise balance of centripetal and centrifugal forces shown in Figure 19 changes over time, either in response to commercial forces or in response to government planning decisions. The interplay of these forces has a major impact on the cycle of urbanisation and the evolution of the city structure and shape.

Review 8

Make a list of the key processes and revise a clear definition supported by an example. The key processes are in bold in Figure 19.

Changing urban environments

Urban morphology

Urban morphology can be defined as the form or internal structure of an urban area — that is, how the various functions found within a town or city are arranged. Often distinct land-use **zones** can be recognised, in which particular functions are concentrated, for example the Central Business District (CBD).

The main reason for this zoning is the cost of land. **Bid rent theory** is often used to explain zoning. It states that all functions have a price they will pay for a certain piece of land within an urban area. For example, in the centre of a city or town, land prices are generally very high. Only land uses such as high-class retailing or prestigious financial institutions can afford these costs (purchase price or rent, and rates) and so 'out bid' other uses such as offices or housing.

Agglomeration is also a significant factor in zoning as many business functions benefit by grouping together within a business/office zone. Increasingly, positions along major road intersections (arterial and radial) are highly prized, and valued by functions requiring maximum access to consumers — for example, car showrooms agglomerate here.

History is a very significant factor in influencing how the settlement developed. Urban areas in MEDCs generally developed from a historic core and spread outwards in a concentric fashion — thus housing is generally older near the centre and much of it can be of poorer quality compared with the newer outer suburbs. In LEDCs there is a marked contrast between urban areas that were **colonial** settlements and those that were not. Ex-colonial settlements always have a high-class administrative area which has now become the focus for a new indigenous elite group.

Specialist site factors influence morphology in a particular way. Many cities have a waterfront area that was traditionally a zone of heavy industry (**break-of-bulk location**). As the function changed, this waterfront area frequently became derelict and later provided opportunities for regeneration (e.g. Cardiff Bay or Albert Dock, Liverpool).

Political factors (both central and local government) play a major part in how land is redeveloped, or developed. Many city planning departments have very strict laws on zoning — controlling where developments can be built.

Tip You need to be able to draw maps to show the morphology of at least one MEDC and one contrasting LEDC, showing the major zones. You can then annotate the maps to describe the land uses, and identify the factors responsible.

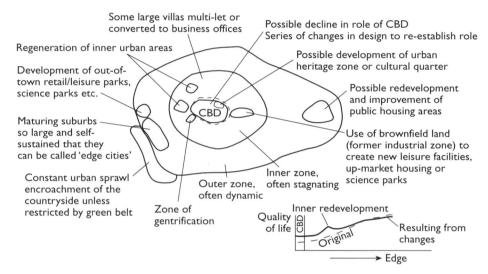

Figure 20 Changes that may be occurring in an MEDC city

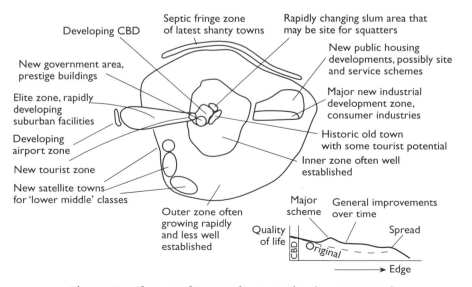

Figure 21 Changes that may be occurring in an LEDC city

Urban areas are constantly changing. Figures 20 and 21 provide checklists for changing urban morphology in an MEDC and an LEDC.

Warning — these diagrams give you some possibilities for change. You need to refer back to examples you have studied and draw an actual map of your case study with precise, named details of changes and their locations. While you may find many of the developments shown, some will be lacking in your chosen example.

Urban models

An **urban model** is a simplified diagram created by looking at a range of cities and then making a generalisation, to include all the similar features. A combination of fieldwork (primary data collection) and map and census analysis (secondary research) can be used. Once you have drawn the model you can then compare it with a city and try to explain why the morphology of your chosen city or town is similar or different. You must choose a model that is appropriate to your chosen city. Some classic models, e.g. Burgess concentric rings, were developed over 80 years ago for circumstances completely different (i.e. very rapid growth) from those experienced in MEDC cities today. Other models, such as the multiple-nuclei model, only apply to cities that are developed from a number of centres — e.g. Los Angeles or Stoke-on-Trent. LEDC cities have had a completely different history from MEDC cities, so again specialist models need to be used. For studying UK cities, especially the northern industrial cities, Mann's model developed in the 1960s (Figure 22) is perhaps the most useful. Another UK model you might find useful is Robson's (based on Sunderland).

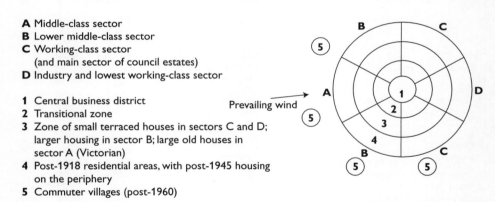

A Middle-class sector
B Lower middle-class sector
C Working-class sector
(and main sector of council estates)
D Industry and lowest working-class sector

1 Central business district
2 Transitional zone
3 Zone of small terraced houses in sectors C and D; larger housing in sector B; large old houses in sector A (Victorian)
4 Post-1918 residential areas, with post-1945 housing on the periphery
5 Commuter villages (post-1960)

Prevailing wind

Figure 22 Mann's urban structure model

How does Mann's model work?
- It has concentric *rings* based on the age of the development as the city spreads outwards.
- It has very obvious *sectors* based on social class.
- The key factor is the prevailing westerly wind, which in the coal-based Industrial Revolution blew smoke eastwards across the city. Thus richer, middle-class housing was found in the west.

- Less-favoured easterly areas were occupied by industry, with adjacent workers' houses (a legacy of the nineteenth century when people had no transport to work). More recently, the outer working-class council estates were found in the unfavoured east. So the cost and status of housing follows a sector pattern.
- The model takes into account the development of the commuter zone in the rural–urban fringe (see **5** in Figure 22).

Issues in the CBD

Figure 23 summarises the key features of a CBD core and frame.

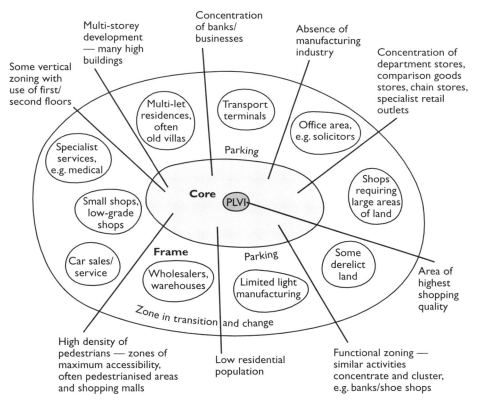

PLVI = Peak land value intersection — the highest rated, busiest, most accessible part of a CBD

Figure 23

Review 9

The CBD of a town or city has a number of key features, shown in Figure 23. As Figure 24 indicates, many factors have encouraged CBD decline. (1) Make a copy of Figure 24 and identify the factors as push (away from the CBD) or pull (towards the periphery). (2) Relate the factors to a local example you have studied.

Rise in car ownership leads to increased personal mobility and the rise of 'leisure' shopping

City centres are perceived as dirty, unsafe, with an ageing environment and poor infrastructure

Planning policies can encourage urban expansion and provide developments 'out of town'

Progressive suburbanisation leads to urban sprawl; for edge cities, the city centre may be many miles away

Factors influencing CBD decline

City councils, determined to attract new industry/inward investment, offer beautiful greenfield sites for development

Congestion means that accessibility of many CBDs is reduced

Companies find peripheral locations cheaper, and nearer the affluent customers and staff who live in the leafy suburbs

Investment in city centres has been largely in prestige projects; it has often lacked a coordinated plan

Investors and businesses are attracted by peripheral sites which have good access and beautiful environments and often lower costs

The costs of development and upkeep of CBDs are high (business rates, rents and land costs)

Figure 24

The changing CBD

Most CBDs in cities in MEDCs are currently under threat for three main reasons:
- the loss of the retailing function to out-of-town shopping centres
- the loss of offices to suburban or peripheral locations in prestige science parks
- the nature of the CBD itself — which because of congestion is becoming increasingly inaccessible, especially as the bulk of the population live in suburban areas. Equally, the CBD has very high rents and rates and is only affordable to prestigious businesses, so the centrifugal forces begin to dominate

Most decision-makers are extremely concerned that CBDs are declining, as there are potentially enormous problems for run-down city centres, which can become very dangerous areas at night. As most people visiting the city arrive in the centre, a run-down CBD could discourage investment. It is easy for 'blight' to set in and whole areas of a CBD to decline. Planners see the CBD as an important social and cultural meeting place and argue that a declining CBD will only accelerate the success of suburban/out-of-town centres. Many of the general public are not convinced about the worth of CBDs and flock in their thousands to shop in retail parks or to work in suburban offices in leafy science parks.

Reviving the city centres

A number of strategies are being devised to help the city centre fight back:
- establishing a business and marketing management team to coordinate overall management of the centre and special events

- pedestrianising the streets in the CBD core to improve safety and to provide a more attractive shopping environment with new street furniture, floral displays, paving and landscaping
- encouraging the construction of all-weather shopping malls/centres (air-conditioned in summer and heated in winter) in key locations in the city centre, often with integral low-cost parking — this latter feature is a controversial issue
- encouraging the development of specialist areas, including attractive open street markets, cultural quarters and specialist arcades selling high-quality products such as organic farm produce or local handcrafts
- improving public transport links right to the heart of the city centre with rapid transit, shopper buses, and park-and-ride schemes
- planning the car parking to ensure ease of access to the city centre, but at the same time controlling congestion (complex schemes can use pricing and length of stay to produce designer car parking)
- making city centres safer places, with video cameras to reduce crime and calm the public's fear of crime
- developing new facilities for leisure and culture — perhaps a new flagship attraction, such as the photographic museum in Bradford (however, not all attractions are successful, as shown by some of the millennium schemes)
- cleaning up shopping centres and buildings and developing a range of tourism activities to encourage greater spending, for example by **conserving the heritage** (shoppers and tourists alike flock to centres such as York, Chester, Cambridge and Bath because they enjoy the ambience)

In the USA, where shopping malls are extremely widespread, the movement to 'bring back and revitalise' the town centres is gathering speed as both planners and the general public realise the dangers of dead city hearts ('urban donuts').

Round the clock city centres

The problem at present in British cities is that their CBDs become 'dead' and dangerous at night. By encouraging shoppers to stay longer and perhaps dine out you can also encourage them to spend more. The following are some possible schemes:

- running shopping events, for example Christmas markets and fairs — late night and Sunday shopping are good options, but they cost money to run and have to be well marketed (e.g. Birmingham)
- encouraging a wider range of leisure facilities, such as café bars, restaurants, music venues, theatres and cinemas, that people would naturally visit in the evening (e.g. Leeds)
- promoting street activity, by encouraging street cafés and street events — realistic only in the summer months in the UK (e.g. Covent Garden, London)
- developing night life — for many cities, such as Leeds or Manchester, 'clubbing' is a major money earner, *but* are the negative effects too great to outweigh the benefits of the trade? (Clearly a high level of policing/surveillance is essential.)
- establishing theme areas, such as the gay area in Manchester, or cultural quarters (Stoke and Sheffield)

- bringing back residential living to the dead heart — either flats to rent above the shops, the development of old buildings (a strand of gentrification) to form upmarket apartments or the actual building of new housing within the city centre (Manchester)

Most CBD managers are trying a range of these strategies and shoppers are being attracted back to centres. However, this can only happen in conjunction with limiting the number of suburban or out-of-town shopping centres and giant super malls, such as the Trafford Centre in Manchester or Blue Water in Kent, by *controlling* planning permission for these.

There are a number of well-documented studies of the impact of these super malls on traditional town centres. Usually the smaller towns are most affected. For example, Merry Hill in the West Midlands has affected Dudley far more than it has Birmingham.

Changes at the rural–urban fringe in an MEDC

Figure 25 summarises the main features of the rural–urban fringe.

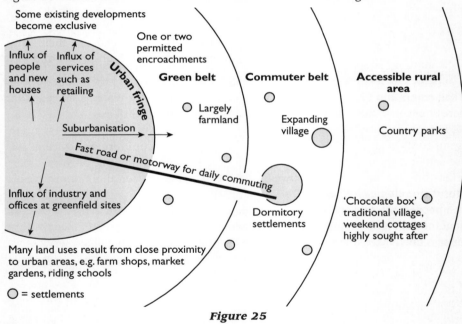

Some existing developments become exclusive

Influx of people and new houses

Influx of services such as retailing

Urban fringe

One or two permitted encroachments

Green belt

Commuter belt

Accessible rural area

Suburbanisation

Largely farmland

Expanding village

Country parks

Fast road or motorway for daily commuting

Influx of industry and offices at greenfield sites

Dormitory settlements

'Chocolate box' traditional village, weekend cottages highly sought after

Many land uses result from close proximity to urban areas, e.g. farm shops, market gardens, riding schools

◯ = settlements

Figure 25

The rural–urban fringe emphasises the concept of the rural–urban continuum. It is very much a zone in transition — a highly desirable zone for which many land uses are competing. Urban sprawl gradually extends into the rural–urban fringe and causes many pressures and conflicts.

(1) The **urban fringe** is a zone of advancing suburbanisation — with high levels of car ownership. High-quality houses on the fringe of the urban area are always in demand — the urban fringe is perceived as quieter, less polluted, more crime-free and less congested, often with access to quality services such as good schools. With

beautiful views of the countryside, living at the urban edge is seen as combining the advantages of town and country living. In general, the homes built there are highly priced and sell well, but as the urban fringe is always advancing (unless it is controlled by a green-belt area) the rural 'idyll' may be an illusion after a few years as the open view disappears and spare land is gradually released for development.

(2) The **green belt** is used in European countries to control urban sprawl. It is an area of open farmland and recreational land around an urban area. Within the green belt it is very difficult to obtain planning permission for new development. The only development that can take place in green-belt areas is within existing villages, by the process of limited infill, or where planners decide the national and regional needs will be met — for example in the creation of a prestigious hi-tech science park that will bring new jobs to an area. In theory, by restricting growth in green-belt areas, developers should be encouraged to use brownfield development sites in inner urban areas. The reality is, because of the higher cost of developing brownfield sites, the developers merely start building beyond the green belt in zone (3), the commuter belt. There is direct map evidence that green belts are being eroded, but they are also very restrictive. Some planning authorities form green wedges or corridors because these allow more development yet also conserve open countryside. Because of their rarity value, any developments in green belts can command very high prices and any housing pre-dating the creation of the green belts soon becomes exclusive.

(3) The **commuter belt** has developed beyond the green belt in response to demand. Where there is a motorway or fast road, large **dormitory settlements** develop, so called because commuters only come home to sleep there. Technically, as these occur in semi-rural areas, they are products of the process of **counterurbanisation**. But these settlements are very suburban with large commuter estates, out-of-town super-markets and leisure facilities. However, in the sectors between the main transport routes, commuter developments are more restricted — often to small estates of six or seven houses, lifestyle hobby farms and renovated country cottages. Here the process is genuine counterurbanisation. Some people move to this zone for retirement but are dependent on establishing their new homes where there are basic village services.

(4) Beyond are the beginnings of a 'tame' rural zone which is very much used by big-city dwellers for weekend recreation. Clearly the areas under most pressure are the attractive *and* accessible areas. **Country parks** have been developed in this zone specifically for day trippers from urban areas. The original idea of these country parks was to take pressure off high-value environmentally sensitive sites in National Parks.

The very mixed nature of the rural–urban fringe is influenced by four main factors: agricultural policies; the nature of the agricultural economy; the urban economy; and countryside planning regulations.

The rural–urban fringe is a mosaic of land use and land types — from high quality to degraded or derelict land — all within a small area. Many land uses look attractive but others look very ugly. As the area is under pressure from competing uses, its state and appearance can change rapidly. Also, many of the land uses, like golf courses, are not very natural and are controversial. Table 9 summarises the best and worst features of this zone.

Table 9

Land use	The good?	The ugly?
Agricultural use	Many well-managed and manicured market gardens and smallholdings	Farms are often fragmented, struggling for survival and frequently suffering litter, trespass and vandalism; some land is left derelict in expectation of planning permission
Development	Some well-sited, well-landscaped developments in the form of business and science parks	Some developments, such as out-of-town shopping areas, can bring heavy pollution; many small-scale, semi-illicit businesses (e.g. scrap metal/junk yards, caravan storage) can arise
Urban services	Some, such as reservoirs or cemeteries, can be reasonably attractive	Others, such as mineral workings, sewage works, landfill sites, and Sunday markets, can be eyesores
Transport infrastructure	Some new green-ways and cycle-ways give access to the countryside	Motorways carve up countryside and promote development
Recreation and sport	Country parks and golf courses can lead to conservation; sports fields provide vital leisure facilities	Some areas can be run down and badly managed, e.g. stables ('horsiculture'); other areas are for noisy sports, e.g. stock car racing and scrambling, which erode the ecosystems
Landscape and nature conservation	High-quality countryside, many SSSIs and AONBs	Much degraded or deteriorating land, e.g. that ruined by fly-tipping; many SSSIs under threat

Conflict results from:

- **commercial decentralisation** — industry seeking rural greenfield sites as opposed to city brownfield sites
- **housing demands** place pressure on the rural fringe — again, a strong desire to build in green-belt areas and attractive villages
- **social differences** between traditional country dwellers and the newcomers — while dormitory villagers put pressure on schools and medical services they rarely use village services such as shops
- **farming** — problems of trespass, vandalism and dogs, where people seeking recreation try to use farmland
- **environmental issues** — much of the development of roads, new science parks and new housing can cause increases in pollution, and also heighten flood risks

Tip An ideal area to study pressures in the rural–urban fringe is anywhere in southeast England, in particular hotspots such as the Silicon Fen near Cambridge, or the M4 corridor.

Inequalities in urban areas

Inequalities are found in all urban areas — in general, the scale of the inequalities reflects both national and regional patterns. What the urban models showed was that enormous contrasts in wealth can often be found over small distances. When you do fieldwork you can actually sense a neighbourhood improving or deteriorating suddenly. Both the wealthy and the poor do seem to concentrate spatially (i.e. **social segregation**), and there are a number of reasons for this.

The key is **housing,** which is 'fixed' in location. Developers, builders and planners tend to build housing on blocks of land with a particular market in mind. Wealthier groups can choose where they live — paying premium prices for areas well away from poor areas, with pleasing environments and quality services such as schools. The poorer groups have no choice and are in a sense forced to live where they are placed in welfare housing, or where they can find a cheap place to rent privately.

Housing is only a partial explanation and needs to be considered in the context of **changing environments**. Housing neighbourhoods change over time — large Victorian villas are now too large for the average 2 + 2 family and so have developed into multi-let apartments for private renting. Other neighbourhoods have improved dramatically because of **gentrification**.

The same type of housing can be built in different environments. It may be on an attractive hillside or in a recently improved neighbourhood and so be targeted by upwardly mobile people. The **right to buy** certainly transformed some council estates, where whole streets of houses were bought and improved.

In many cities there is a further **ethnic** dimension. Originally, ethnic groups are new immigrants to the country. They often suffer discrimination in the job market and are either unemployed or employed in low-paid jobs. They are not able to afford to buy anything other than very cheap housing (inner-city terraces), or have to rent privately (not on council housing lists). Therefore, newly arrived migrants concentrate in poor areas in the city, often clustered into ghettos for cultural reasons, and such ethnic groupings tend to persist.

Measuring inequalities

It is possible to measure the **quality of life** in an area using primary data such as the quality, density and condition of housing, and the nature of the environment (physical and social). Levels of pollution or crime are good indicators here (see Figure 26).

It is also possible to use secondary data from a census to assess **deprivation** levels — this may include **poverty** in terms of low income or manifested in poor health or lack of possessions such as cars. It is very common for the poorest parts of an urban area to suffer from **multiple deprivation** — with social, environmental and economic deprivation. There have been many indexes devised to measure deprivation, including Townsend's (shown on page 81).

Urban social exclusion is a recent term which refers to the problems faced by residents in areas of multiple deprivation. Essentially, these people are excluded from full participation in society by their social and physical circumstances. They cannot get access to a decent job because of poor education, or obtain decent housing because of poverty, and have to suffer high levels of crime and poor health in a very unattractive physical environment.

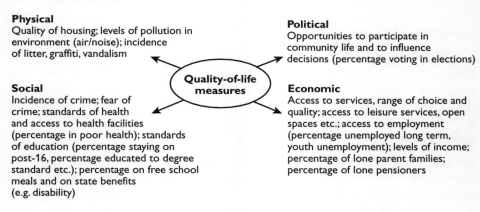

Physical
Quality of housing; levels of pollution in environment (air/noise); incidence of litter, graffiti, vandalism

Political
Opportunities to participate in community life and to influence decisions (percentage voting in elections)

Quality-of-life measures

Social
Incidence of crime; fear of crime; standards of health and access to health facilities (percentage in poor health); standards of education (percentage staying on post-16, percentage educated to degree standard etc.); percentage on free school meals and on state benefits (e.g. disability)

Economic
Access to services, range of choice and quality; access to leisure services, open spaces etc.; access to employment (percentage unemployed long term, youth unemployment); levels of income; percentage of lone parent families; percentage of lone pensioners

Figure 26

Tip Early 'headline' results of the 2001 census should be available by December 2001. Get in there fast and use up-to-date figures in your case studies.

Inequality can have major consequences in a city in terms of a lack of social cohesion. In extreme cases it can lead to civil unrest. Clearly governments have to address social injustices for a variety of social, economic and political reasons. Figure 27 shows an idealised quality-of-life transect across a city in the UK.

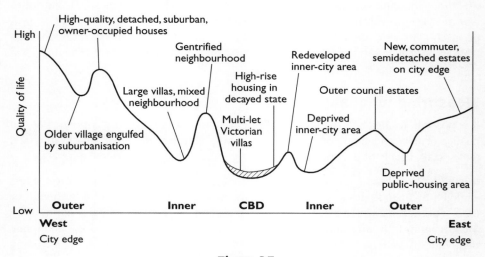

Figure 27

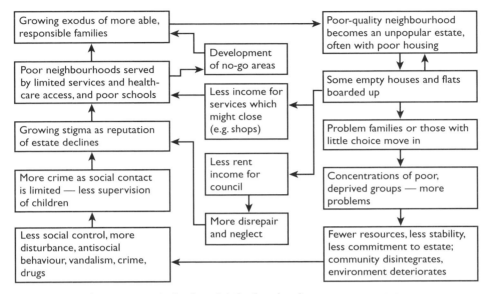

Figure 31 Spiral of multiple deprivation on poor estates

Internal factors — those within ethnic groups that encourage segregation

New arrivals need mutual support from friends, relatives and community organisations

These immigrants will be happiest with religious centres, ethnic shops and foods, and banks grouping together to serve them

These immigrants need support from areas speaking their own language — a minority language in their new country

These ethnic groups encourage friendship and marriages and reduce contacts, except via schools, which might undermine the culture and traditions of the ethnic groups

Employment and accommodation can often be obtained via networking in an ethnic community

A closely knit ethnic community provides security against abuse and racist attacks — safety in numbers

Ethnic groupings help political power and influence development

External factors — those within the country or area that encourage ethnic segregation

As immigrants move in, the remaining majority population moves out — in fear of factors such as falling house prices

The majority population is generally hostile or unfriendly to new arrivals

Racism, abuse, racially motivated violence against ethnic minorities or fear of such actions

Discrimination in the job market — ethnic minorities in low-paid jobs or unemployed are forced by circumstances into cheap housing areas and substandard services

Discrimination by house sellers, estate agents and housing agencies keeps ethnic minorities in their ghettos

Discrimination by financial institutions forces ethnic minorities to use their own networks for small business development etc.

Ethnic segregation in urban areas leading to concentration

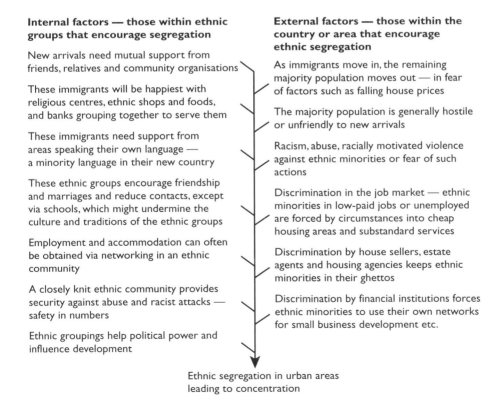

Figure 32 Factors encouraging ethnic segregation

Ethnic clustering is a complex topic and patterns of ethnic groupings vary.

In cities where immigrants are long established, well integrated and not threatened by racial documentation, they tend to be dispersed throughout the city as their confidence and affluence increases. This has happened in Sydney and Melbourne and is known as **mixing**. Multinational plurality prevails.

In many other cities, such as Los Angeles, particular ethnic groups are concentrated in different parts of the metropolis, but not for the same reasons. Figure 33 shows these contrasts.

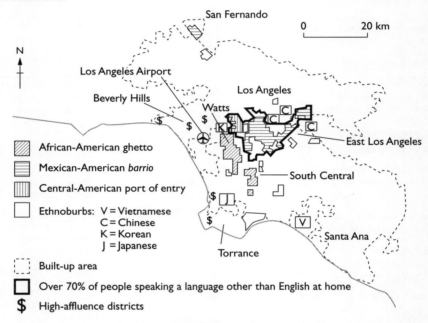

Figure 33 The ghettos of Los Angeles

- Some concentrations occur in the central area, such as the African-American ghetto in Watts in central Los Angeles. Sometimes this has been for historic reasons where there were large quantities of cheap housing to rent or to buy. In other cases concentrations are in poor-quality social housing areas in the suburbs.
- Recent immigrants, such as Mexicans, have concentrated in *barrios* in, for example, East Los Angeles and San Fernando. They may leave these *barrios*, as they secure better jobs and learn the language, but will not do this if they feel racially threatened or discriminated against.
- Figure 33 also shows what can be called the **ethnoburbs** of Pacific Rim immigrants. These are middle-class or professional immigrants who settle in relatively affluent suburbs, where they invest in businesses and develop their properties. These new clusters are for choice, convenience and cultural reasons and are often influential economic enclaves.

authorities, such as prestige tourism projects, cultural quarters or Millennium schemes (e.g. the Welsh National Stadium).

Three trends emerge from this case study:
- the increasing role of central government decision-making
- increasing private investment — usually after public investment 'pump-priming' or on a 'matched' funding basis
- increasing movement away from social schemes as the focus, with economic consensus seen as the key to improvement (although in 2000 it is moving back to social issues of health and education)

The success of urban regeneration can be evaluated against a number of criteria, in particular:
- were the objectives of any particular scheme met?
- were the targets reached within the allocated period of funding?

Figure 35 sets out an evaluation framework. You should use this for your chosen urban regeneration schemes (e.g. Cardiff Bay and London's Docklands).

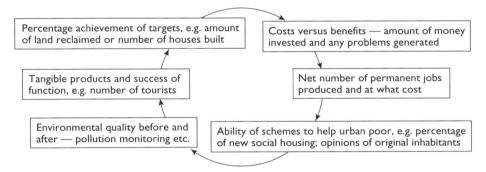

Figure 35 Evaluation framework for urban regeneration

While there have been spectacular successes and cities such as Glasgow and Birmingham have transformed their images, a number of concerns have been expressed about regeneration in many cities, especially that carried out via the Urban Development Corporations (e.g. London Docklands).

Regenerating and redeveloping urban environments in LEDCs

In LEDC cities and towns the key issue is the **Brown Agenda**, a mix of social and environmental problems brought about by rapid growth and industrialisation associated with economic development. One danger for students is to overemphasise the problems of these cities, especially the mega-cities, at the expense of the whole range of efforts from governments and NGOs to improve the conditions of the large numbers of people living below the poverty line. You will study a number of LEDC cities and towns and your aim should be to research a range of improvements made. Most standard textbooks focus on at least one city, such as Mexico City, Cairo or Bangalore.

NGO strategies for poverty reduction include:

- promoting new yet appropriate technology — for example, solar panels, mini-hydros, or fuel-efficient stoves
- provision of credit and training to empower local entrepreneurs — often the potential of women is under-recognised
- strengthening local organisations, through support for local networks and developing community-led (bottom-up) projects such as the Healthy City projects or local Agenda 21 projects. Some of the networking can be between countries of the North and South, but South to South is likely to be more beneficial.

These micro-approaches can contrast with the more top-down approaches of local authorities which largely provide infrastructural improvements. Some of these schemes, such as the renewal of Cairo's sewers, are financed via international aid programmes or by UN agencies. At a macro-scale, international governments try to provide an institutionalised framework (e.g. for trade) to control urban poverty. Many transnational corporations (some more powerful financially than the LEDCs they operate in) also contribute to a number of urban improvement projects.

Sustainable cities — planning for the future

Cities, particularly the mega-cities of the world, can be regarded as unsustainable in a number of ways. For example:

- they 'suck in' and consume enormous quantities of resources — food, energy, water, raw materials from the surrounding regions and (for an MEDC city) even from all over the world
- they produce enormous quantities of waste, which are dumped in the surrounding land, rivers (ultimately oceans) and the atmosphere

Urban environmental sustainability can be defined as meeting the present needs of urban populations in such a way as to avoid harming the opportunities for future generations to meet their needs. This can only be achieved by organising and managing cities:

- to minimise damage to the environment
- to prevent the depletion of natural resources

The Rogers models shown in Figure 36 compare an unsustainable city with a sustainable city.

Note the differences in the amount of inputs and outputs, and the important roles of recycling and pollution control in the sustainable city. Some cities, such as Curitiba in Brazil, are models of sustainability, i.e. **green cities**. Others, such as London or Los Angeles, have much work to do.

Sustainability can be considered in a wider context of economic and social sustainability:

- **economic** sustainability allows individuals and communities to have access to a reliable income

- **social** sustainability provides a reasonable quality of life, and opportunities to maximise personal potential. Many inhabitants of the world's cities do not have access to these rights, which can be clearly linked to environmental sustainability.

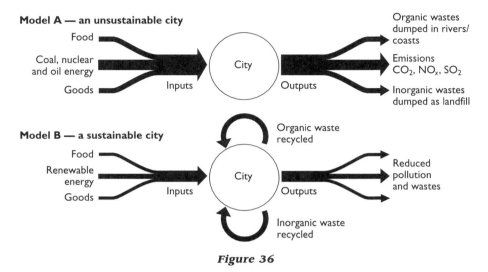

Model A — an unsustainable city

Food

Coal, nuclear and oil energy

Goods

Inputs

City

Outputs

Organic wastes dumped in rivers/ coasts

Emissions CO_2, NO_x, SO_2

Inorganic wastes dumped as landfill

Model B — a sustainable city

Food

Renewable energy

Goods

Inputs

City

Outputs

Organic waste recycled

Reduced pollution and wastes

Inorganic waste recycled

Figure 36

Sustainable cities would be:
- less damaging to the global environment, for example by slowing global warming or ozone depletion
- developing a higher-quality urban environment with access to serviced housing and adequate open spaces
- providing greater opportunities for their citizens to enjoy a reasonable quality of life free from poverty, with equality of opportunity and access to healthcare
- allowing the freedom to participate in decision-making that concerns their cities

In terms of **management**, a number of options exist for all cities (see Figure 37).

In terms of design, **compact** cities would reduce the distances people have to travel to services, facilities and work. They would use less space by building more intensively, at higher densities. There would also be a need to develop mixed zoning in neighbourhoods — usually called urban villages — comprising a mixture of housing, employment, shops, services and leisure facilities to reduce car travel and encourage walking and cycling.

A compact city would be easier to manage than a sprawling city:
- it would be easier to provide its infrastructure — pipes, cables etc. would run shorter distances, while higher-density buildings could be cheaper to heat
- it would be easier to develop public transport because of a more concentrated market — thus reducing reliance on the private car
- it would be easier to develop more viable services because of a more concentrated market — for example district shopping centres

- it would allow people to enjoy a full range of facilities on their doorstep without the inevitable car journey
- if built on derelict brownfield sites it would cut down on urban sprawl into green-field sites — thus making it more sustainable

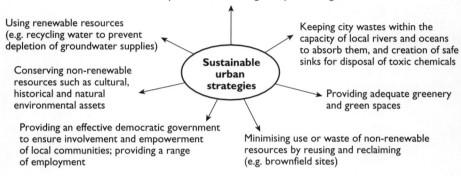

Getting to grips with energy use, by reducing reliance on fossil fuels — in particular, rethinking transport management

Using renewable resources (e.g. recycling water to prevent depletion of groundwater supplies)

Conserving non-renewable resources such as cultural, historical and natural environmental assets

Sustainable urban strategies

Keeping city wastes within the capacity of local rivers and oceans to absorb them, and creation of safe sinks for disposal of toxic chemicals

Providing adequate greenery and green spaces

Providing an effective democratic government to ensure involvement and empowerment of local communities; providing a range of employment

Minimising use or waste of non-renewable resources by reusing and reclaiming (e.g. brownfield sites)

Figure 37

However, in European and North American countries there is strong opposition to the notion of compact cities — high density is equated with congestion, overcrowding and lower-quality housing with a lack of personal garden space, perhaps increasing stress and noise levels. Compact sites are an essential design for sustainability, but are hard to sell even in LEDCs — Shanghai turned down a compact city design in preference to a conventional sky-scraper model dominated by the private car.

Agenda 21, an agreement set up at the Rio Earth Summit in 1992, provides a frame-work for local authorities to develop sustainable strategies. A typical 'shopping list' would include:
- promoting energy efficiency
- greening the city by landscaping streets etc.
- establishing effective recycling of waste/litter etc.
- introducing quality public transport and provision for walking/cycling
- promoting green growth to provide employment
- monitoring existing levels of pollution to improve standards

Many cities have moved to develop sustainable features. Curitiba in Brazil is always cited as a shining example of sustainability in action and is considered to be an eco-city. Sustainability projects are also widespread in LEDC cities as Agenda 21 is a global framework (see **www.iied.org/eandu** for examples).

Tip Look at a range of Agenda 21 strategies for your local town and suggest how they would lead to greater urban sustainability. Be optimistic — urban areas may have many problems, but a great deal of energy, expertise and enterprise is being channelled into making them fit places for people to live in.

Questions
&
Answers

In this section of the guide there are three questions based on the topic areas outlined in the Content Guidance section. Each question is worth 30 marks. You should allow 30 minutes when attempting to answer a question, dividing that time according to the mark allocation for each part.

The section is structured as follows:

- Three specimen questions are presented, similar in style to those in the Edexcel B papers. These illustrate typical questions (2), (3) and (4) (see page 5). Remember, there will be five to choose from in the real examination.
- Answers have been provided to the short-answer questions, showing you how to squeeze the maximum marks out of data response in order to achieve an A grade.
- For the long-answer questions, an answer of A-grade standard and an answer of C-grade standard have been provided so that you can see the reasons for the difference in achievement. Using examples and case studies is a vital part of these long-answer questions, and the A-grade standard answers show you how to do this.

Examiner's comments

Candidate responses to long-answer questions are followed by examiner's comments, preceded by the icon ℮. They are interspersed in the answers and indicate where credit is due. In the weaker answers, they also point out areas for improvement, specific problems and common errors such as poor time management, lack of clarity, weak or non-existent development, irrelevance, misinterpretation of the question and mistaken meanings of terms.

The comments indicate how each example answer would have been marked in an actual exam. For questions with only a few available marks, examiners generally give each valid point a mark (up to the maximum possible). For higher-mark questions, examiners use a system involving 'Levels':

Level 1 At this level, answers generally contain simple material. Points are stated briefly with no development. Examples are given in one or two words, usually in the form 'e.g....', and explanation is basic, such as 'A is the cause of B'.

Level 2 Answers at this level need to contain more detail. For instance, if the question requires a comparison, a Level 2 answer will contain some quantification, such as 'A's GDP is 10 times larger than B's'. Examples are more detailed and explanations involve clearer reasoning: 'A is the cause of B because...'.

Level 3 This is the highest level. Marks are awarded for breadth and depth, for drawing together the threads of a response and for overall evaluation.

Changing rural environments

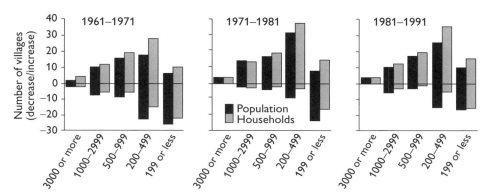

Figure 1

(a) Figure 1 shows population and household change by parish size in Breckland, East Anglia.

  (i) Describe the changes in parish size in 1961–71. (3 marks)

  (ii) State *three* differences between the changes shown for 1961–71 and those shown for 1981–91. (3 marks)

  (iii) Suggest reasons for *two* differences you have identified in (ii). (4 marks)

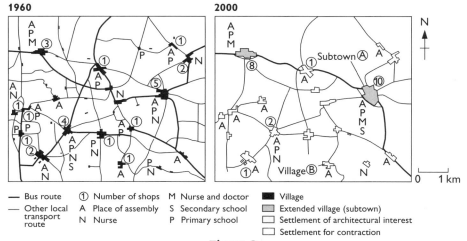

—	Bus route	①	Number of shops	M	Nurse and doctor	■	Village
—	Other local transport route	A	Place of assembly	S	Secondary school	▨	Extended village (subtown)
		N	Nurse	P	Primary school	☐	Settlement of architectural interest
						☐	Settlement for contraction

Figure 2

(b) Figure 2 shows changing service provision for a rural area of eastern England in 1960 and in 2000.

  (i) Briefly describe how the service provision changed between 1960 and 2000. (4 marks)

  (ii) Assess the impact of the changes in service provision on:
  - a family living in subtown **A**, both parents working, three teenage children
  - a pensioner living in village **B** (6 marks)

question

(c) Many rural areas experience rural deprivation. Explain what is meant by rural deprivation and identify some possible solutions. (10 marks)

Total: 30 marks

■ ■ ■

Answers to parts (a) and (b)

(a) (i) • For large settlements — 2 decreased, 2 increased
   • For 1000–2999 people — 10 increased, 8 decreased
   • For next size 500–999 — most increased but a few decreased
   • For 200–499 — 18 increased, 23 decreased
   • For the smallest size (under 200) — 5 increased but 26 declined
   • For household size there was more increase overall and less decrease than for the population

   e 1 mark for each, up to a maximum of 3. It is a good idea to try to give an overview and include a full range of points to be sure of achieving full marks. Use precise numbers where they are available rather than general terms such as 'less decrease' and 'more increase'.

(ii) • In 1981–91 overall there was much greater increase, especially of larger settlements.
   • In 1981–91 the largest settlements all increased (in 1961–71 some declined).
   • In 1981–91 the smaller settlements declined a lot less.

   e Three valid differences given, for maximum marks.

(iii) • Expansion of the larger settlements may have been designated as key settlements, with better services, improved employment and therefore much housing infill.
   • Overall increase is probably associated with counterurbanisation whereby urban people are moving from the towns into the countryside. This is facilitated by commuting potential, teleworking and improved lifestyles.

   e 2 × 2 marks for two valid reasons. Always be sure to write extended/developed reasons using geographical terminology, as above.

(b) (i) The subtowns have increased their shop numbers (up to 10) while:
   • overall, nine shops have closed
   • many bus routes have been axed (only main route left)
   • a health centre has opened but many villages have lost their nursing provision
   • five primary schools have been closed, but a secondary school has opened
   • most villages have retained their community halls

   e Four valid points for 1 mark each. Remember to quantify amounts in such questions; don't use terms such as 'many' and 'most' if you can give a figure. Be careful to include growth and decline.

(ii) • A good level of service is likely, with more shops (probably a key settlement) — healthcare and a secondary school are useful for teenagers. The family is essentially better provided for. A by-pass improves the town centre environment.
  • A pensioner is likely not to be a car driver (but may be). A designated settlement for contraction has lost nursing services, meaning a trip of 3 km to a doctor, and even 2 km for a pension and village shops (since the pensioner's village lost its basic shop). Note — it was always a remote area, and the continued availability of the village hall suggests that events like luncheon club, bingo and 'bright hour' might still be available.

🖉 2 × 3 marks. With 6 marks for two reasons you must develop your points and support your answers with data, linking them to the people in the question.

Answer to part (c): average candidate

(c) Rural deprivation can occur in areas such as south Shropshire, where rural people are deprived of access to services such as banks, and a supermarket within reasonable travelling distance. As many rural areas, particularly remote ones, are very sparsely populated, it is not economic to supply these high-level services. The situation is made worse because rural public transport, such as buses, have declined, and people need a car to get to even basic services such as doctors and banks. This expense, combined with the high price of fuel, means that some poor people, like farm workers or the very old, cannot afford these costs, hence the vicious cycle of deprivation.

There are many solutions but some require a lot of money. One solution, tried in Norfolk, is the idea of key settlements so that everybody has a right to basic services within 3 miles of where they live. Another solution is to think of imaginative and new ways of providing services like village taxis and dial-a-ride, or making post offices into banks and internet access points. Targeting those who need help most is a good idea too. A example of this is the moped hire scheme for young workers in Bishops Castle.

🖉 This essay achieves a mid-Level 2 mark of 6 out of 10. Deprivation is defined in basic terms, with a good description of what it means to people. There is some use of terminology. The candidate offers some solutions, but locations are not given for all the examples.

Answer to part (c): A-grade response

(c) Rural deprivation has three main facets: household deprivation, opportunity deprivation and mobility deprivation. Household deprivation occurs when households live at poverty levels, as a result of low incomes. Many rural dwellers live in property with below-average facilities, and have to rely on just their pension. It is best solved by providing affordable housing in villages. It is also worth ensuring that the people who need the benefits understand what is available and how to apply for them. In a survey of Moreton we found around 20 pensioners, as well as farm workers, who said they were on income support.

Opportunity deprivation is the lack of access many rural dwellers face to a range of services, such as shops and doctors, and also the lack of opportunities to get appropriate or quality employment. It is best solved by imaginative approaches to providing rural services, such as multi-function centres, mobile shops, cyber post offices and also ensuring at least weekly access to the key settlement with a supermarket, bank, health centre etc. Also, a range of rural employment opportunities can be developed through rural tourism or craft workshops. In Moreton we found people who had to travel 5 miles to the nearest supermarket. There was very little employment in the village.

Mobility deprivation is the problem of having no access to the services because of the lack of public transport and the inability to afford a car or private transport. It is best solved by a range of subsidised, quality services including bus partnerships, community dial-a-ride schemes, village shared taxis or mobile services. For some young people, moped hire/lease is an option for getting to work, for example in the South Shropshire Scheme.

e This is a well-structured and informed answer, which defines deprivation clearly, and scores a good Level 3 mark of 9 out of 10. It demonstrates the use of terminology and provides detail and examples. For examples, try the Countryside Agency website at **www.countryside.gov.uk**.

Q2

Rural–urban issues

Table 1

Urban population (millions)

Region	1950	1970	1990	2000	Estimated 2020
The world	2516	3698	5292	6261	8504
Industrialised countries	832	1049	1207	1264	1354
Developing countries	1684	2649	4086	4997	7150
Continents — Africa	222	362	642	867	1597
Continents — North America	166	226	276	295	332
Continents — Latin America	166	286	448	538	757
Continents — Asia	1377	2102	3113	3713	4912
Continents — Europe	393	460	498	510	515

(a) **Table 1 shows the urban population of the world by region.**
   (i) **Describe the trends of the world urban population growth from 1950 to 2000.** (2 marks)
   (ii) **Suggest reasons for the variations between the industrialised countries and the developing countries in urban population growth during the period 1950–2000.** (5 marks)
   (iii) **Summarise the main features of the projected urban population growth for the period 2000–2020.** (4 marks)

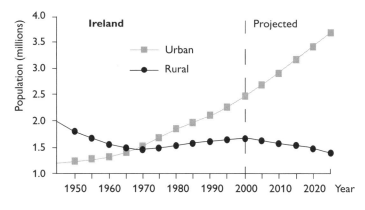

Figure 1

(b) **Figure 1 shows the changing balance of rural and urban population for Ireland.**
   (i) **Analyse the trends shown in Figure 1.** (4 marks)
   (ii) **Outline the implications of the projected trends shown (2000 onwards) for planners and decision makers in:**
   • **rural areas**
   • **urban areas** (5 marks)

question

(c) Describe and suggest reasons for the conflicts that result from the competition for land at the rural–urban fringe.

(10 marks)

Total: 30 marks

■ ■ ■

Answers to parts (a) and (b)

(a) (i) The world population is growing all the time, exponentially (ever increasing).
  - It rose 1200 million in 1950–70 and 1600 million in 1970–90.
  - It then increased by 1000 million in 10 years (1990–2000).

e 1 mark is awarded for the idea of growth and a further mark for data evidence or technical description of the trend. Remember to always quote and interpret evidence.

(ii) • Industrialised countries grew steadily until 1990.
  - They have now levelled off as a result of a balance between birth rates and death rates leading to a low natural increase.
  - In small areas there has been out-migration from urban areas to rural areas, known as counterurbanisation, which has added to the slowing growth of urban areas.
  - Developing countries are increasing exponentially — population explosion.
  - This results from a declining death rate and a continuing high birth rate.
  - In most developing countries there is rapid and recent rural-to-urban migration which has led to very high growth rates as many migrants are aged 20–35.

e This 5-mark question is likely to be marked in Levels. To achieve a Level 3 mark you need to have a balance *between* the two groups of countries, with an extended explanation using geographical terminology and data. This answer easily achieves 5 marks.

(iii) Projected world growth is still exponential with no sign of levelling off.
  This continued growth is because of the very rapid growth in developing countries, which is very numerically dominant in Asia and Africa where the growth is so rapid. In Europe and N. America the increase is slow and that influences the slow growth in the industrialised countries.

e 1 mark for the initial statement, 1 mark for amplification and 2 marks for description/extension. Try to include data from all regions and outline the linked relationships.

(b) (i) • Initially, pre-1950, around 60% lived in rural areas (2.0/3.25), but the rural population declined to 1.4 million in 1970 and was actually less than the urban population.
  - Between 1950 and 2000 the urban population rose steadily from 1.2 to 2.4 million.

- While there was a slight revival in rural population (1990–2000), it is projected to decline to under 1.5 by 2030.
- In contrast, urban population is projected to rise at the same rate to just under 4 million.

e **4 × 1 marks.** For full marks the answer must include rural, urban, actual and projected data. The command term 'analyse' involves making detailed calculations — for example you can work out the percentage rural and percentage urban by adding up the totals to give an overall figure. Use the data, actual and projected, and be comprehensive.

(ii) • Planners are dealing with a steady decline — this may mean there is a need to 'stem' out-migration, for example by supporting rural enterprise/tourism. Services will be more expensive to provide as there will be fewer users (e.g. schools).
- The steadily growing population may place pressure on the supply of housing and provision of other services (education/health). There may be the need to manage urban sprawl, and traffic congestion may be a major problem.

e **2 or 3 marks** are available for either answer, up to a maximum total of 5. Detailed, developed statements are required for full marks, while examples might be useful.

Answer to part (c): average candidate

(c) The rural–urban fringe is under threat as cities such as Birmingham try to expand into the countryside. Many cities have green belts around them to try to curtail urban sprawl. There are major conflicts because people who live on the edge of cities do not want visual intrusion and pollution from increased traffic flow. They see the green belt as land for recreation (e.g. walking) and also as beautiful countryside to look at.

When urban dwellers go out into the rural–urban fringe their action can cause conflict with farmers — for example leaving gates open, damaging walls or allowing dogs to savage sheep.

If the land is not protected green belt, it faces enormous pressures from developers to build out-of-town facilities, executive housing and new science parks. The new facilities generate enormous quantities of traffic.

In some rural–urban fringe zones, existing villages expand tremendously as homes for commuters (e.g. Ashwell). There is often conflict between the old villagers and new villagers. In particular, they have very contrasting ideas on leisure pursuits.

e It is a good idea with questions like this to start with a 1 minute brainstorm to get a simple plan. The candidate has clearly identified four conflicts but they are not always well linked to competing land uses. Exemplification is of the 'e.g.' type. For an A grade you need to develop your examples in detail, for example, naming a specific green-belt site, such as Bassetts Pole, near Sutton Coldfield, and explaining what it is to be used for (in this case a premium industrial site). Also, the language is quite basic, and little geographical terminology is used. The candidate gains a mid-Level 2 mark of 6 out of 10.

Answer to part (c): A-grade response

(c) The rural–urban fringe is a zone of change. As urban areas sprawl outwards, the open countryside gradually comes under threat from new building. In some areas, such as Pendleside (the rural–urban fringe around Burnley and Nelson in Lancashire), a green belt has been designated in which building can only take place if permission is given for exceptional reasons. Such reasons include the need to locate a prestigious pharmaceutical firm, as happened in the green belt area west of Morpeth.

Even with a green belt there are conflicts, especially where urban people walk their dogs on farmland, or take short cuts across fields, breaking down fences. Recently, near Fence, there was a case of a dog savaging seven sheep. Another conflict concerns fly tipping — many urban dwellers dump old cars and other refuse in fields.

There is an enormous variety of land use within the rural–urban fringe, with some high-quality intensive fruit farming, but also some low-quality farming, such as the farms near Heddon on the Wall where pigs are just kept for a few days before being sold to the abbatoir. Many farmers realise that there is the potential to sell up for building land, so they are just waiting for this to happen and don't invest in their farms, leaving them run-down and untidy.

In some areas there is enormous controversy over the building of new golf courses on farmland, for example in Betley, overlooking Stoke. Some people want this recreational facility, but others argue the ecological value of the land will decrease.

In areas such as Bassetts Pole, where the new Birmingham relief road is being built, the rural–urban fringe is under constant threat from development. Even the green belt area on the western edge of Birmingham is to be used as a premium industrial site.

Each year around 50 hectares of attractive farmland are lost to out-of-town developments such as retail parks and executive homes. In many villages, such as Sutton, there is conflict between the new arrivals and the traditional villagers. There is also great concern about traffic congestion in the country lanes.

e This is a full response, using some terminology and describing a range of conflicts in named locations. It scores a low Level 3 mark of 9 out of 10, failing to score full marks through an apparent lack of planning or structure.

Urban environments

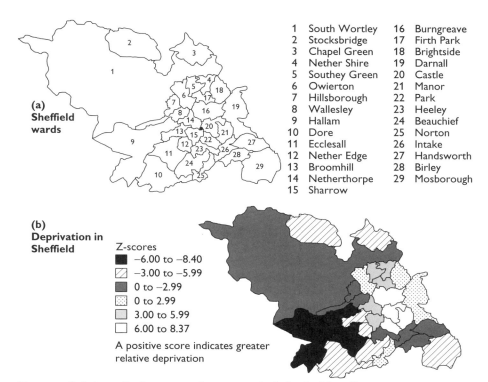

1	South Wortley	16	Burngreave
2	Stocksbridge	17	Firth Park
3	Chapel Green	18	Brightside
4	Nether Shire	19	Darnall
5	Southey Green	20	Castle
6	Owierton	21	Manor
7	Hillsborough	22	Park
8	Wallesley	23	Heeley
9	Hallam	24	Beauchief
10	Dore	25	Norton
11	Ecclesall	26	Intake
12	Nether Edge	27	Handsworth
13	Broomhill	28	Birley
14	Netherthorpe	29	Mosborough
15	Sharrow		

(a) Sheffield wards

(b) Deprivation in Sheffield

Z-scores
- −6.00 to −8.40
- −3.00 to −5.99
- 0 to −2.99
- 0 to 2.99
- 3.00 to 5.99
- 6.00 to 8.37

A positive score indicates greater relative deprivation

Townsend's index criteria were used to create the index in (b):

(1) percentage of economically active adults who were unemployed, January 1997
(2) percentage of households on income support, December 1996
(3) percentage of all children in households with no earners, December 1996
(4) percentage of households without a car, 1991
(5) percentage of households not owner-occupiers, 1991

Figure 1

(a) Figure 1 shows the location of Sheffield wards and the pattern of deprivation in Sheffield using Townsend's index.

(i) Describe and suggest reasons for the distribution of levels of deprivation in Sheffield:
  - in the best areas
  - in the worst areas (6 marks)

(ii) Comment on the good and bad features of the indicators used in Townsend's index. (4 marks)

(iii)State two types of fieldwork evidence you could collect to assess deprivation in urban areas. (2 marks)

3

question

A Middle-class sector
B Lower middle-class sector
C Working-class sector
  (and main sector of council estates)
D Industry and lowest working-class sector

1 Central business district
2 Transitional zone
3 Zone of small terraced houses in sectors C and D;
  larger housing in sector B; large old houses in
  sector A (Victorian)
4 Post-1918 residential areas, with post-1945 housing
  on the periphery
5 Commuter villages (post-1960)

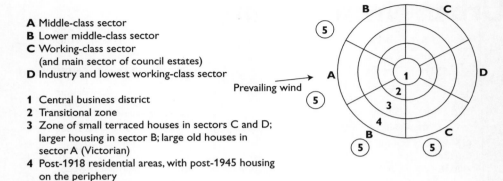

Prevailing wind

Figure 2

(b) **Figure 2 shows Mann's model for a British city.**
  (i) **What principle is used to draw the concentric rings?** (2 marks)
  (ii) **What principle is used to define the sectors?** (2 marks)
  (iii) **Suggest two ways in which the model is similar to Sheffield (Figure 1).** (4 marks)
(c) **With reference to a named large urban area in an LEDC, describe and explain
  the distribution of its most deprived areas.** (10 marks)

Total: 30 marks

■ ■ ■

Answer to question 3

(a) (i) ● The areas of relative advantage are found in the southwest towards the outer
  edge, but some stretch towards the centre (possibly gentrified villas). The
  rest are likely to be owner-occupied suburban dwellings (1950s onwards) for
  relatively affluent people with cars, likely to be working in a range of professional, managerial jobs.
  ● The most deprived wards, Manor, Park, Castle and Burngreave, are concentrated in the inner city, east of the CBD. These could be inner-city terraced
  housing areas, or possibly local authority postwar housing (tower blocks etc.)
  found in a solid cluster. They may well be former industrial areas with de-
  industrialisation leading to high unemployment, with many households on
  income support.

  e 3 marks are available for each part (2 × 3) — 1 for names/identification, 2 for
  reasoning and development — so it is important to include description, named
  examples, location and at least two reasons linked to Townsend's index.

  (ii) For:
    ● They are up-to-date (even 1996). 1991 is the last published census.
    ● They do concentrate on poverty and economic deprivation.

Against:
- There is a raft of social statistics such as health/education levels, which might give a broader picture — Townsend's index only uses five indicators.
- The percentage of owner occupiers may be a suspect indicator because you can rent at any level of income.

e There are 4 marks here so be sure to make four clear points and bullet them for clarity or alternatively give two developed points. (Mention good *and* bad features equally for full marks.)

(iii) • Assess the housing condition using a random sample and a housing quality survey sheet.
- Assess the environmental quality using a street condition survey sheet.
- Could also do questionnaire on people's opinions.
- Access to services (basic shops/doctors).
- Percentage of green open space.

e Any two for a maximum of 2 marks.

(b) (i) Age — the city developed in concentric rings over time, with the oldest areas in the centre and the youngest on the fringe.

e 2 marks — 1 for age and a further mark for the extension.

(ii) Social class/income — the impact of the prevailing SW wind means that the middle-class sector is found up-wind from the industrial zone whereas the poor, who have no choice, are found down-wind in the east.

e 1 mark is awarded for a factor, the other mark for extension. There is more detail here than needed for full marks.

(iii) • Sheffield shows the wedge of advantage in the southwest, stretching from Hallam to Dore inwards towards Eccleshall.
- Sheffield also shows the concentration of low-class deprivation (strongly polarised) in the east (Castle, Manor etc.), although it does not extend out to the edge towards Darnall.

e 2 marks are awarded for each of the two reasons. Always use located examples.

Answer to part (c): average candidate

(c) My chosen large city is Lima in Peru. In general, the quality of life is better nearer the town, especially in the western sector of Miraflores, because this is where the oldest shanty towns are, so they now have sites with services and paved streets.

There are, however, one or two very poor areas of inner-city slums where new migrants come. Here there are very high densities in very run-down houses. On the bed of the River Rimac there are spontaneous settlements of squatters, with some of the city's poorest people living in makeshift houses. They are at risk from flooding. Other very poor areas include the squatter settlements at the very southern edge of Lima, where the new migrants from the country have just arrived. They have no services, and the area is very dusty because there are no paved roads and it is on the edge of a desert. Another very poor area is down by the port, where the industrial area is mixed with squatter settlements. These squatter settlements are called favelas.

e This is a mid-Level 2 answer, gaining 5 or 6 marks out of 10. While it is clearly about Lima, more detail of locations is required (a map would have helped). However, there was no need to include details of richer areas such as Miraflores. The explanations show some understanding but also some inaccuracies.

Answer to part (c): A-grade response

(c) My chosen large urban area is Cairo — located 200 km from the north African coast, south of the Nile Delta. With between 11 and 14 million inhabitants, this mega-city is by far the largest in Africa. Cairo has large, poor residential areas. These include the old areas found in central Cairo, which are extremely crowded (with many people living on the rooftops), as well as large areas of shanty towns, such as Fustat and those that extend out towards Giza, covering some rich agricultural land. The distribution of these very poor areas is shown on the map below.

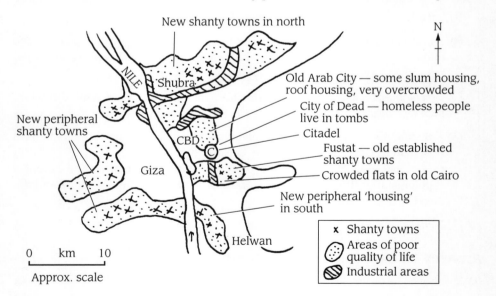

Cairo is growing at a rate of 300 000 per year, largely as a result of rapid rural-to-urban migration. It is this which has led to an enormous expansion of shanty towns (for locations see map) which extend into the desert area. Many are on very unfavourable ground, located next to factory zones. Many of these settlements do not have services (water, electricity etc.).

The old town is, in effect, a slum area with population densities of over 100 000/km². Squatters settle in simple shelters on roof-tops, and housing is frequently substandard. The desperation for accommodation in Cairo has led to the colonisation of the city's cemeteries by homeless families — known as City of the Dead — which provides shelter for up to 1 million people in tombs.

The local authorities try to provide basic services for all these areas, which make up nearly half the city.

The candidate has produced a grade-A answer for the following reasons. It is very well linked to Cairo with a useful map (don't be afraid to draw diagrams over lined paper in the test). The description is very precise, with named locations, while the distribution is *partially* explained. Overall, the candidate scores 10 out of 10 marks at Level 3.